easter treats

easter treats

recipes and crafts for the whole family

by jill o'connor
crafts by mikyla bruder
photographs by jonelle weaver

CHRONICLE BOOKS
SAN FRANCISCO

Library of Congress Cataloging-in-Publication Data:

O'Connor, Jill.
 Easter treats : recipes and crafts for the whole family /
 by Jill O' Connor; crafts by Mikyla Bruder; photographs by Jonelle Weaver.
 p.   cm.
 Includes index.
 ISBN 0-8118-2384-9 (pb)
 1. Easter Cookery. 2. Easter decorations. 3. Handicraft. I. Title.
 TX739.2.E37026 2000   99-10118
 641.5'68—dc21   CIP

Printed in Hong Kong.

All crafts by Mikyla Bruder except Secret Message Easter Eggs,
 Japanese Washi Eggs, and Easter Collage Box, by Jill O'Connor.
Prop styling by Christina Wressel
Craft styling by Maggie Hill
Food styling by Bettina Fisher
Design and illustrations by Carrie Leeb, Leeb & Sons

The photographer wishes to thank the following people for their hard work: Bettina Fisher, food stylist; Barb Fritz, prop stylist; Josh Zuckerman, assistant; Tina Rupp, prop assistant; and Elissa Levy, production coordinator.

Distributed in Canada by Raincoast Books
8680 Cambie Street
Vancouver, British Columbia V6P 6M9

10 9 8 7 6 5 4 3 2 1

Chronicle Books
85 Second Street, San Francisco, California 94105

www.chroniclebooks.com

Notice: This book is intended as an educational and informational guide. With any craft project, check product labels to make sure that the materials you use are safe and nontoxic. Nontoxic is a description given to any substance that does not give off dangerous fumes, or contain harmful ingredients (such as chemicals or poisons) in amounts that could endanger a person's health.

The Art & Creative Material Institute in Boston certifies nontoxic supplies. Look for their seal of approval on art and craft product labels. For a complete product list of nontoxic brands (as well as those to avoid), write or call the institute at 100 Boylston Street, Suite 1050, Boston, MA 02116; Phone: 617-426-6400.

For Mom and Dad, for pink heart-shaped pancakes on Valentine's Day, Christmas morning mimosas, and biscotti-jar Easter baskets. Thank you for all the love you poured into creating special holiday traditions that will shine in my memory forever.

My daughter was born three months after I completed my first book, *Sweet Nothings*, and stood by my side, literally, as I tested the recipes for my second book, *Phyllo*. She is my most enthusiastic taster and never stops telling me what a good "cooker" I am. So it is with pleasure that I write this book, filled with recipes and crafts kids will love to help create.

Every book I write depends on a great deal of input and assistance from my family and friends and the goodwill and confidence of my editors at Chronicle Books. Thank you to Leslie Jonath, who never expressed any doubt about my finishing this project, even as I was moving from Hawaii to Rhode Island, and who has always encouraged my efforts. My friends have always been enthusiastic supporters of my writing endeavors, and I would like to express special thanks to Denise Kuhn, who read the manuscript and gave me so much helpful and kind advice, and who taught me how to create the beautiful *washi* eggs; Lori Francini, who could give Martha Stewart a run for her money, for her tips on the cookie pops; and Mary Ann Kelly, who continues to impress me with the joy and patience she brings to motherhood, and who always laughs at my jokes. We all need a friend just like her.

Most of all, I want to thank my husband, Jim, who has been my champion from the beginning of my culinary and writing career and never once told me I was insane to start working on this book in the middle of a major move across the country. I can't imagine any other husband who would take a break from writing his thesis to assist with the construction of an Easter bunny cake. I thank him—and his engineering acumen—for helping me construct that difficult bunny haunch.

Finally, thank you to my parents, my brothers, and all my friends and family who have taken such an interest in this and all my other books, and who continue to cheer me on. I truly appreciate and love you for it.

table of contents

here comes peter cottontail...

Tips of purple crocus push their way through the last drifts of winter snow. Buttery daffodils crack through the cold of winter and turn their happy faces toward a warming sun. Tender shoots of grass are at their most brilliant green. Spring is here! Easter, one of the most joyous holidays in Christianity, celebrates the resurrection of Christ. The Easter season is also a time when we honor the unity of our family and friends, welcome spring, and revel in the awakening beauty of nature after the long days of winter.

Children look forward to dyeing and decorating eggs in bright colors, and devouring the chocolate bunnies, jelly beans, and candy eggs left in their Easter baskets by the elusive Easter bunny. The holiday bunny hopped into American folklore with German immigrants who settled in Pennsylvania Dutch country in the 1700s. German children built nests of hay or grass in their caps and bonnets, and placed them in secluded areas of their homes and yards in hopes that the bashful bunny would reward their kindness by filling the nests with colored eggs and sweets. Baskets later replaced the traditional caps, and by the end of the 1800s, the Easter bunny and his basket of brightly colored eggs had become an integral part of the Easter celebration in America.

But children are intrigued by more than bunnies and baskets on Easter morning. Indeed, they love the anticipation and preparations for Easter as much as the holiday itself. It is a perfect time to include them in planning and preparing the feast and creating special decorations for the Easter table. With your help they can turn plain tin cans into colorful containers to hold tulips, or fashion an Easter Egg Tree from a flowering branch on which to hang their favorite decorated eggs.

To get in the spirit of the season, host an egg-decorating party or a cookie-decorating party for your children and their friends a day or two before Easter. Boil eggs and dye them by the dozen. Bake egg-, rabbit-, or basket-shaped cookies ahead of time. Set out small bowls of assorted decorations and allow the kids to flex their artistic skills by painting the cookies with colorful icings, or gluing glitter and ribbons to the boiled eggs. The kids can proudly serve their cookies with Easter brunch, nibbling on them after a busy morning spent hunting for their glorious eggs.

No Easter celebration would be complete without a meal with family and friends. The menus in this book showcase the bounty of spring as well as the traditions of Easter. Elegant and delicious, creamy risotto brimming with smoky pieces of grilled asparagus celebrates the seasonal harvest. Spicy, buttery hot cross buns, first prepared in Great Britain on Good Friday and marked with a cross by superstitious housewives to ward off evil, are a delicious and traditional addition to an Easter brunch. Decorative crafts such as Little Violet Vases and Easter Votives are simple and elegant homemade additions to your Easter table.

The jubilant feelings celebrated during this season are shared by many. Easter is a joyous holiday, a festival of hope and renewal, and a time to rejoice with family and friends. Throw open your windows, breathe in the sweet scent of spring, and celebrate.

how to use this book

To inspire you and your children with the spirit of this wonderful season, this book is divided into three sections. First comes *Easter Fun*, which includes instructions for boiling, blowing, dyeing, and decorating the perfect Easter egg, covering them in delicate Japanese washi paper or adorning them with pretty ribbons. A recipe for sugaring flowers in anticipation of creating delicious Easter sweets is also included here. The second section, *Easter Feasts*, includes three delicious menus for Easter Brunch, Easter Luncheon, and Easter Dinner, all with recipes to entice children, family, and friends. Interspersed are decorating ideas that sparkle with springtime cheer. Finally, *Easter Sweets and Treats* delivers a basket of treats with recipes for a playful Easter Bunny Cake, colorful Chicken Little Cookie Pops, and delightful crafts such as tiny Fuzzy Chicks made with pom poms. Throughout the book, you'll see violet-colored illustrations, signifying that this craft is simple enough for little ones to accomplish with minimal supervision.

More than anything else, as you prepare the recipes and crafts presented here, enjoy your child's desire to be with you, to help you, and to participate in your preparations for Easter. Your child will be building happy memories and absorbing many valuable lessons in math, language, listening, and patience as he or she cooks and crafts with you. So, praise your child's achievements, encourage their willingness to help, and enjoy the sweet fruits of his or her labor when you are both done.

Happy Easter!

cooking and crafting with kids

Cooking and creating crafts with children is a wonderful opportunity to take advantage of their natural enthusiasm. Following are some practical tips to help keep cooking and crafting fun, safe, and kid-friendly.

keep it safe

* The first thing to remember when cooking and crafting with young children is safety. Limit young chefs (ages four to six) access to the stove top and oven, and save stove-top stirring for older children who are taller, steadier on their feet, and more experienced. Keep pot handles away from the stove edge, to prevent passersby from bumping them.

* Make sure hands are washed with warm soapy water and dried completely before cooking begins, and long hair is tied back to keep cooking safe and sanitary.

* Use only safe tools. Keep sharp knives, scissors, or heavy equipment out of their reach. Offer children under six plastic knives or small flexible icing spatulas for cutting soft vegetables like mushrooms. For crafts, offer blunt-edged scissors, nontoxic and washable paints, markers, and glue. Glue guns are for adults only!

* Place a damp dishcloth between the cutting board and the countertop. This keeps the cutting board steady for chopping.

* If children are going to help stir, whisk, or even use a handheld electric mixer, make sure the bowl is sturdy enough and large enough for the task. A bowl that is too small is hard to handle, even with an adult involved.

* Although taste-testing is one of the joys of cooking, avoid licking the beaters of cake batters, cookie dough, or other dishes containing raw egg. Salmonella is still a real threat.

* Eliminate roughhousing! Remind young children that scissors are not toys, and that running while cooking or crafting is neither safe nor allowed.

keep it clean

* Cleaning vegetables is a great task for children under six. Help them rinse lettuce and spin it dry in a salad spinner. Give them a soft vegetable brush to clean mushrooms or strawberries.

* Have a pile of clean, wet sponges and a roll of paper towels handy for spills and quick cleanup along the way.

* Cover your table with an inexpensive vinyl or oilcloth tablecloth. For a work surface that is big and easy to clean, it's a small investment that saves your table and your sanity.

* Slip a big, old T-shirt on your young chef and artist, instead of an apron or smock. It covers everything, is easy to find, and is easy to wash.

* Children love to crack eggs, but it's a messy business. To keep eggs from landing on the floor, have your child gently tap the middle of the egg on the rim of a bowl and then help as he or she separates the halves over the center of the bowl. Discard the shell and have children wash their hands immediately after handling raw eggs.

* Laminate recipe cards for easy cleanup. Start a collection of recipes and craft ideas your family enjoys making. Use colored pens and pencils to decorate the cards before laminating them. Purchase an inexpensive recipe box and let your young chef decorate it.

keep it simple

* First things first: remember your child's attention span and plan a project accordingly. Start with short, easy recipes and crafts and work your way up to larger tasks. Small children love routine and familiarity, so start building family food traditions they will enjoy preparing for years to come.

* Take a tip from professional chefs and get your *mise en place* in order. This French term simply means to set out the ingredients and equipment you need for the preparation of a specific dish before you begin cooking.

keep it fun

* Have a supply of child-sized utensils handy. Good-quality wooden spoons, rubber spatulas, and metal whisks are available in smaller sizes perfect for child-sized hands, and small spreaders are ideal for a variety of tasks, from cutting vegetables to spreading icing on cookies. For crafting, child-sized scissors, thick crayons, and easy-to-hold glue sticks are always handy to have around.

easter fun

easter eggs

Early Christians adopted the egg as a symbol for Easter, and for centuries, artisans from many countries have lovingly crafted and decorated beautiful eggs to celebrate the holiday. You, too, can flex your creative muscles and design wonderful decorated eggs. Host a decorating party and organize workers into an assembly line to blow, boil, and dye a big batch. Then gather everyone around the table with the dyed eggs, glue, glitter, ribbons, stickers, sequins, beads, buttons, and bows and let the artistry begin. Here are tips for boiling, blowing, and dyeing eggs as well as fun decorating ideas that produce festive results.

the perfect hard-boiled egg

1 dozen eggs

1 teaspoon salt

Boiling the perfect egg isn't difficult, but it does take patience. Cooking the eggs at a low simmer will make them easier to peel and help prevent cracks. Cool immediately after cooking to eliminate the unattractive grayish green circle that can form around the yolk. These hard-boiled eggs can be used immediately, or dyed and decorated and featured first in your Easter egg hunt and later as deviled eggs.

Place the eggs in a single layer, without crowding, in a 2- or 3-quart saucepan. Add water to cover by 2 inches and then the salt. Bring to a boil over high heat. Reduce the heat to low and simmer for 15 minutes.

Immediately remove the eggs from the hot water and plunge them into a basin of very cold water to cool down, or rinse under cold running water for about 5 minutes.

To peel, roll the large end of the egg on a countertop to crack the shell. Hold the egg under cold running water, and peel away the shell. Store unpeeled hard-boiled eggs in the refrigerator until ready to use.

blowing the eggs

Pierce the fat end of a raw egg with a large needle, such as a quilting needle. Wiggle the needle to create a slightly larger hole. Pierce a hole in the opposite end of the egg. Insert the needle to pierce the yolk; this makes it easier to remove the egg. Use a baby's nose aspirator to "blow" the contents of the egg into a large bowl. When the egg is empty, run water into the eggshell, shake it to rinse the insides well, and pour it out.

dyeing the eggs

To make each dye bath, stir together ⅛ teaspoon paste food coloring with 1 teaspoon distilled white vinegar in a small bowl or nonporous coffee cup. Add 1 cup boiling water and stir to dissolve the food coloring fully.

Add 1 egg to each dye bath. A blown egg will float at first, but as you gently press it into the dye bath with a spoon, it will take on liquid and begin to sink. Allow the egg to sit in the dye bath for about 10 minutes for the most intense color.

Remove the egg (drain any liquid inside the egg back into the dye bath). Repeat this process with the remaining eggs. Allow to dry completely before decorating.

ribbon eggs

For each ribbon egg you will need:

various ribbons and trims

small paintbrush

craft glue

1 blown egg, dyed or plain

scissors

tiger tail (miniature wire cable available at craft or bead stores) or thin cord

2 beads or tiny buttons (large enough to cover the holes in the egg)

glue gun

Eggs festooned with pretty pieces of ribbons are surprisingly easy and very beautiful. Use ribbons that are fairly narrow, 1/4 inch or less. Rickrack and other narrow trimmings work well, too. Explore the notions section of your fabric store for interesting textures and patterns. There are no rules, so have fun.

Select the ribbons you want to use. Brush a thin, even layer of glue on one side of the ribbon, and wrap around the eggshell. Snip away extra ribbon.

Fold an 8-inch length of tiger tail or thin cord in half to form a loop. Thread the ends of the loop through a bead or a small button and tie to secure, retaining a loop at the top of the bead or button. Using the glue gun, glue the bead over the hole at the top of the egg, making sure that the tiger tail knot is inside the egg. Glue another bead or button over the bottom hole.

easter egg tree

To create an Easter tree, anchor a tree branch in a pail or bucket filled with small stones or marbles (available at gardening stores). If your branch is blooming, pour water over the stones. Use Christmas ornament hooks, ribbon, or cord to hang decorated eggs such as Ribbon Eggs (above) or Starry Sky Eggs (page 26). Bags of candy and lollipops are also good ornaments for your trees.

secret message easter eggs

For each message egg you will need:

paintbrush

1 blown egg

craft glue or glue pen

glitter

scissors

airmail stationery or tracing paper

pen with gold, silver, or other colored ink

sequin, sticker, or other decoration

crafter's glaze (optional)

These glittery eggs, with a message tucked inside each one, are fun for children and adults alike. Instead of glitter eggs, you can create collage eggs by cutting out small decorative accents from wrapping paper, gluing them to the egg, and then glazing the decorated egg with crafter's glaze for a shiny finish. You can also attach sequins or feathers with water-based glue or affix decorative stickers.

Brush the entire egg with a thin coating of craft glue and sprinkle with glitter, for jeweled eggs. Alternatively, use a glue pen to draw decorative designs and sprinkle them with glitter.

For the fortune or note, cut out a 2-inch by 2-inch square from a sheet of airmail stationery or tracing paper. Write a love note, or a fortune, roll up tightly and slip into the larger hole on the bottom of the egg. Cover the hole with a sparkly sequin, sticker, or other decorative accent. The recipient cracks the egg to discover the message.

If the eggs are too beautiful to crack, make the hole in the top of the egg a little larger with a quilting needle, roll the note very tightly, and insert it, leaving a little bit exposed so it can be pulled out without destroying the egg.

bunny ears

Dress up your little ones with these easy-to-make ears. You should handle the glue gun, but the kids will love to wear the finished product. If you can't locate craft foam, you can make these ears out of construction paper, but they won't be as sturdy.

Cut out a paper or cardboard template of a 6- to 8-inch bunny ear, with a pointed tip and squared-off bottom.

Fold the white craft foam in half crosswise. Place the base of the ear template along the fold and trace around the outside of the ear. Repeat. Cut out the 2 ears. Don't cut through the fold. Each ear will have a front and a back. Using the glue gun, take one ear and glue the front to the back, making sure to leave an opening near the base large enough to accommodate the headband. Repeat with the other ear. Slip the headband through the openings at the base of each ear. If it doesn't fit snugly, apply more glue around the base of the ears and pinch tightly around the headband.

Using scissors, trim the cardboard template $1/2$ inch all the way around. Place this small "ear lining" template on the pink craft foam and trace around the outside of the ear lining. Repeat. Cut out the 2 ear liners. Glue them to the fronts of the ears. Allow to dry thoroughly before wearing.

For each set of bunny ears you will need:

$8^{1/2}$-by-11-inch sheet cardboard

scissors

pen or pencil

11-by-17-inch sheet white craft foam

glue gun

white plastic headband (available at craft or fabric stores)

$8^{1/2}$-by-11-inch sheet pink craft foam

japanese washi eggs

For each *washi* egg you will need:

origami paper

string

scissors

1 blown brown egg

rice starch (either powdered or gel form)

2-inch paintbrush

small sponge

craft glaze, varnish, or lacquer (water-based, nontoxic type)

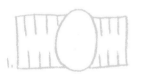

*Japanese origami paper (*washi *means "paper" in Japanese) and rice starch are available at craft and art supply stores. Be sure to ask for the heavy-grade paper. When you turn it over you should see the fibers running through it. Wooden eggs, available in craft stores, can be used in place of blown eggs. Kids might also find it easier to create a collage egg, using small pieces of origami paper, applying them randomly, and then glazing the egg.*

The goal is to cut a paper rectangle that wraps around an upright egg and covers it from top to bottom. Use a piece of string to measure the circumference of the egg at its middle, and a second piece to measure it from top to bottom. Use these two measurements as length and width and cut out the paper rectangle.

Cut perpendicular slits along each long side of the rectangle, spacing them about 1/2-inch apart and leaving an uncut band 1/2- to 1-inch wide down the length of the center. Next, cut on each side of the paper strips to form pointed tips. The finished rectangle will have picket-fence-like strips on each side and an uncut band down the center.

Prepare the rice starch according to package directions. Brush it over the entire egg and on the back of the rectangle. Center the uncut band of the paper horizontally on the egg and wrap the paper around the egg, pressing to smooth out any wrinkles (see diagram). If the paper is not centered correctly on the egg, it can be safely lifted off and repositioned. Pull all the paper picket-fence strips away from the egg. Starting with one strip, press it gently to the egg from the center of the paper to the tip. The tip should reach the hole in the end of the egg. Smooth out any wrinkles with your finger or a small, barely damp sponge. Repeat with the next paper strip, overlapping the first strip

slightly, and then with the remaining strips on that end. When completed, turn the egg over and repeat with the strips on the opposite end. If the strips are too long and overlap the tip, trim them to a point farther down. If too much wrinkling occurs near the center of the egg, cut the strips down a little farther into the center band.

Allow the egg to dry completely (a blow dryer can speed up this process). For a shiny finish, brush the egg with crafter's glaze, varnish, or lacquer. Again, allow to dry completely.

easy easter daisies

These sunny daisies look good almost anywhere. Glue them to your Easter basket, stitch the daisies around the edge of a table runner, or pin them to a ribbon and use the ribbon to tie back a curtain or a little one's hair.

Photocopy or trace the daisy on this page and cut out the template. Cut out the center circle and discard. Position the template in the corner of the piece of white felt. Using the fabric pen or pencil, trace around the petals. Repeat until you have traced 12 daisies on the white felt.

Now position the template in the corner of the piece of yellow felt. Using the fabric pen or pencil, trace the center circle. Repeat until you have traced 12 circles on the yellow felt.

Using scissors, cut out the felt flowers and circles. Glue the felt circles to the center of the flowers. Repeat until you have 12 finished flowers. Allow the glue to dry thoroughly before using.

For 1 dozen daisies you will need:

flower template (see this page)

pen or pencil

small, sharp scissors

8$\frac{1}{2}$-by-11-inch sheet white felt

fabric pen or pencil

8$\frac{1}{2}$-by-11-inch sheet yellow felt

craft glue

starry sky eggs

For each starry sky egg you will need:

1 egg, hardboiled or blown

12 small star-shaped stickers

blue egg dye or paste food coloring

distilled white vinegar

hot water

small paintbrush

craft glue

clear or silver glitter

Stars sparkle against a blue backdrop on these pretty eggs. Look for star-shaped stickers in art or office supply stores. Purchase small stickers in other interesting shapes, such as tiny flowers, hearts, or geometric shapes, and use this same technique to create different looks.

Affix the star-shaped stickers to the egg. Mix the dye with vinegar and hot water, according the instructions on the egg dye package or to the paste food coloring instructions on page 17. Double or triple the amount of dye for a deeper shade of blue. Dye the egg, following the instructions on the dye package, and allow to dry thoroughly.

Remove and discard the star-shaped stickers. Carefully paint each white star with craft glue and sprinkle with the glitter. Allow to dry.

chicken feed

4 cups (one 7-ounce can) crisp shoestring potatoes

1 cup salted corn nuts

1 cup shelled sunflower seeds

1½ cups dried blueberries

1 cup shelled pistachio nuts

1 cup unsweetened coconut flakes (broad shavings) available in natural food stores

This barnyard-inspired snack mix is a crunchy, nutty trompe l'oeil treat. Indeed, you might even be tempted to scatter it to the chickens, but save it for yourself instead. It takes minutes to assemble and is the perfect snack to satisfy hungry little egg decorators. Young cooks can help measure the ingredients and then toss them together in a large bowl with a wooden spoon or with freshly washed hands. Serve this crispy nibble in a burlap-lined basket to continue the barnyard theme.

Makes 9½ cups

Combine all the ingredients in a large bowl and toss lightly to combine. Serve immediately or store in a lock-top bag for up to 1 week.

candy cones

Good art supply and craft stores sell decorative craft papers by the sheet in various sizes. Use a heavier gauge paper for these cones, so they'll last longer. Hand the cones out at the egg hunt, or surprise a child by filling a paper cone with candy and hanging it on her bedpost or doorknob early Easter morning. When Easter is over, fill the paper cones with dried flowers or bunches of dried herbs.

Using the scissors, trim the craft paper to a 12-inch square. Trim one edge of the square with the pinking shears, if using. Bring two opposing corners together and roll the paper into a cone, with the pinked edge overlapping the plain edge. Glue the edges together. You can use paperclips to hold the cone together until it's dry.

Using the scissors, carefully trim away the top corner of the paper, leveling out the rim of the cone. Punch holes on either side of the cone, about 1 inch below the rim. Thread the grosgrain ribbon through the holes and tie to secure, forming a handle.

Glue lengths of rickrack and assorted ribbons or a row of daisies around the cone.

For each candy cone you will need:

scissors

ruler

1 sheet heavy craft paper, at least 12 inches square

pinking shears (optional)

craft glue

$1/8$-inch-hole paper punch

grosgrain ribbon, 12 inches long and 1 inch wide

rickrack and assorted ribbons or Easy Easter Daisies (page 25)

easter egg basket

For each basket you will need:

newspapers

wicker basket with handle

white spray paint

small paintbrush

tempera paints in pastel shades

clear acrylic spray (optional)

assorted silk flowers or Easy
  Easter Daisies (page 25)

glue gun

ribbon

green tissue paper

scissors

For a personalized, traditional Easter basket, explore your favorite art supply and craft stores for a plain wicker basket. Dress it up with a fresh coat of paint, silk flowers or handcrafted Easter daisies, and ribbon. Little ones can assist in trimming their own baskets, but adults should handle the spray paint and the glue gun. The optional clear acrylic spray will give the basket a longer life.

Select a work surface outdoors or in a well-ventilated area, and cover it with newspapers. Place the wicker basket on the newspapers and spray paint it. Allow to dry.

Select details on the wicker basket, such as the rim, the handle, and strips around the center, and use the small paintbrush to paint the details in pastel colors. Allow to dry. If desired, spray the basket with the clear acrylic spray. Allow to dry thoroughly before decorating.

Remove stems from silk flowers. Using the glue gun, place a bead of glue at the base of an artificial flower or an Easter daisy, and glue the flower to the basket. Repeat with as many more flowers as desired. Wrap a length of ribbon around the handle and tie to secure at each end.

To make "grass," fold a sheet of green tissue paper lengthwise three times. Snip off thin strips crosswise to form the grass blades. Repeat as needed until you have the desired amount of grass. Fill the basket with the grass, making a soft resting place for eggs and candy.

sugared flowers

Toni Elling, a lovely woman in upstate New York, transforms tender flower blossoms into delicate, crystallized jewels. Her company, MeadowSweets, sugars almost any edible flower, from violets, violas, and pansies to rose petals, primroses, and herb blossoms. You can use sugared flowers to garnish White Chocolate Truffles (page 87), Easter Bonnet Shortbread Cookies (page 72) and other Easter sweets. Young children can help sprinkle the sugar over the blossom while an adult holds the flower steady. Use only pesticide-free edible flowers, and sugar as many as you can in one sitting. Stored in a cool, dry place, they will keep for several months.

Make sure the flowers are clean and completely dry. Trim off the stems with scissors. Working with one flower at a time, grasp the stem end with tweezers. Brush the flower with the egg white (or reconstituted meringue powder), covering the front and back of each petal completely. Holding the flower over a plate, sprinkle with superfine sugar, making sure to cover both sides of each individual petal generously. Place the flower on the waxed paper and allow to dry for at least 2 hours. If the weather is humid, the drying may take longer. Make sure they are light and crisp before using.

Store the sugared flowers in a single layer in an airtight container. Keep in a cool, dry place out of direct sun until ready to use.

Note: Toni Elling contends that lavender is edible, but strongly flavored, so she recommends these for nonedible garnishes only. Violets, the most popular flowers to sugar, are also one of the most delicate and difficult to do. Start with hardier blossoms, like rose petals, primroses, and pansies, and tackle the violet after you have had a little practice.

see photo on page 23

2 dozen pesticide-free edible flowers such as violets, violas, pansies, rose petals, primroses, rosemary blossoms, and/or lavender (see note)

small scissors

tweezers

small watercolor paintbrush (use a new one and reserve for flowers only)

2 egg whites, lightly beaten, or 4 teaspoons meringue powder mixed with $\frac{1}{4}$ cup warm water

dinner plate

2 cups superfine sugar

waxed paper

jelly bean bags

For 8 bean bags you will need:

1 pound miniature jelly beans, assorted colors and flavors

8 squares white netting, each 9 inches square

8 lengths ribbon, each 6 inches long

These little bags of candy can be scattered about the house or yard for children to hunt down. You can substitute different candies, such as candied almonds, gumdrops, and gumballs. Kids will love to fill the bags with candy and tie them up (and nibble as they work).

Place 1/4 cup jelly beans in the center of 1 netting square. Bring the corners of netting together, and tie up the bag with a length of ribbon. Repeat with remaining netting squares, candy, and ribbon.

marzipan play dough

2 tubes (7 ounces each) marzipan

paste food coloring of choice, in 4 colors

Sculpting marzipan is an art form among many pastry chefs, who create a variety of exquisite fruit, flower, and animal shapes to use as decorations. Your children can hone their sculpting skills, forming bunnies, chicks, eggs, or other Easter shapes. Simple sculptures like eggs or mice can be partially dipped in melted semisweet chocolate and served as candy, or a menagerie of marzipan creatures can adorn cupcakes or a simple layer cake. Marzipan is available at most grocery stores.

Divide both tubes of marzipan in half, placing each portion in a small bowl. Knead a few drops of food coloring into each portion until the color is evenly blended. Shape the marzipan into Easter shapes. You can also roll the marzipan out and cut into shapes with miniature cookie cutters. To make marbleized colors, carefully press small pieces of 2 or 3 different colors together and roll out or mold into shapes. Don't knead together too firmly or the colors will be muddied. As the tiny sculptures are formed, place them on waxed paper and allow to air dry and firm up. Marzipan sculptures can be prepared up to 2 or 3 days before Easter and stored in a tightly covered container.

easter feasts

easter brunch for family and friends

After spending the early hours of Easter morning hunting for hidden eggs and munching on too many chocolate bunnies, settling down for a relaxing and bountiful morning brunch is a delicious way to celebrate the holiday with family and friends. The centerpieces of the meal are a glorious whole ham slathered with a rosy glaze and a flaky potato strudel, pungent with garlic and fresh herbs. The bread basket is filled with traditional hot cross buns and nontraditional cornbread madeleines laced with leeks and pecans. A sunny carrot salad tossed with a spicy orange vinaigrette rounds out the savory courses. There are true mimosas for the adults to sip and a child-friendly version for children to enjoy. A simple fruit fool concludes the feast.

Many of these recipes can be prepared in advance, allowing the cook to enjoy the morning festivities. The hot cross buns can be baked and frozen ahead of time and simply thawed and iced before serving, and the carrot salad can be made a day in advance. You can puree the rhubarb-mango mixture up to two days before the party, chill it, and fold the puree into the freshly whipped cream just before serving. Assemble the strudel while the ham is baking. You will be relaxed and happy as you greet your guests, anticipating their enjoyment of this splendid meal.

baked ham with raspberry and dijon mustard glaze

Save the ham bone for soup and use the leftover ham in sandwiches. A little bit of cold ham fried on a nonstick griddle and eaten with a few hot corn bread madeleines makes a tasty snack late in the afternoon long after all your brunch guests have gone home.

Serves 8 to 10, with leftovers

Preheat the oven to 350° F.

Puree the berries with their juices in a blender or food processor, and pass the puree through a fine-mesh sieve. You should have about 1 cup puree.

Stir together the raspberry puree, red currant jelly, and Dijon mustard in a saucepan over medium heat until the jelly dissolves. Raise the heat to high and bring to a boil. Cook, stirring constantly, for 1 minute. Remove from the heat and set aside to use as glaze. You will have 3 cups glaze.

Place the ham, fat side up, in a large roasting pan. Peel off the skin and trim the fat to a layer 1/4 inch thick. Score the fat in a diamond pattern, and rub the brown sugar over the surface.

Roast the ham for 30 minutes. Remove from the oven and pour the water over the ham. Spoon 1 cup of the glaze over the ham, and return it to the oven. Bake for 2 1/2 hours longer, basting every 15 minutes with the pan juices and 1/3 cup of the raspberry glaze (until the glaze is gone).

Line a large platter with fresh kale leaves and parsley sprigs and place the ham on it. Carve at the table.

1 package (12 ounces) frozen unsweetened raspberries, thawed

1 jar (16 ounces) red currant jelly

1 jar (8 ounces) Dijon mustard

1 precooked bone-in whole ham, 10 to 13 pounds

1 1/2 cups firmly packed light brown sugar

1 cup water

kale leaves and flat-leaf parsley sprigs

garlicky red potato strudel

3 pounds small red potatoes, unpeeled

2 tablespoons olive oil or unsalted butter

1 leek, white and pale green part only, well rinsed and thinly sliced

2 or 3 large cloves garlic, crushed

2 cups heavy cream

1/8 teaspoon ground nutmeg

salt and freshly ground pepper to taste

1/2 cup minced fresh herbs, including chives, flat-leaf parsley, and a few mint leaves

10 sheets phyllo dough, thawed in the refrigerator if frozen

1/2 cup (1 stick) unsalted butter, melted and cooled

about 7 tablespoons fine dried bread crumbs

Almost a meal in itself, this delicious accompaniment to ham is a nice change from the more usual potato gratin or scalloped potatoes.

Serves 8 to 10

Preheat the oven to 375°F.

Put the potatoes in a large pot and cover with lightly salted water. Cover and bring to a boil over high heat. Uncover and boil until tender when pierced with a knife, 10 to 15 minutes. Drain and let cool.

Heat the olive oil or butter in a saucepan over medium heat. Add the leek and sauté until limp, 2 to 3 minutes. Add the garlic and cook briefly until fragrant but not brown. Pour in the cream, reduce the heat to medium-low, and cook, stirring occasionally, until slightly thickened and reduced, about 15 minutes. Stir in the nutmeg and season with salt and pepper. Remove from the heat and let cool.

Cut the cooled potatoes into 1/4-inch-thick slices and toss together with the cooled cream and the herbs.

Lay 1 phyllo sheet on a flat work surface, keeping the remaining sheets covered with waxed paper topped with a damp towel to prevent them from drying out. Brush lightly with melted butter and sprinkle with 2 teaspoons of the bread crumbs. Top with a second sheet, brush with butter and sprinkle with 2 teaspoons bread crumbs. Repeat with the remaining phyllo sheets, bread crumbs and most of the remaining butter to create a single stack. Spoon the potato mixture in a strip down a long side of the phyllo, positioning it 2 inches from the edge. Fold the uncovered edge over the filling and roll the phyllo around the filling as you would a jelly roll; pinch the ends closed. Place the

strudel, seam side down, on a parchment-lined baking sheet and brush lightly with the remaining melted butter. Bake until golden brown and the filling is hot and bubbly, about 30 minutes. Let cool for 2 to 3 minutes. Using a serrated knife, slice the strudel on the diagonal into 8 to 10 slices. Serve immediately.

matchstick carrot salad with cumin-orange vinaigrette

1 pound large carrots, peeled and cut into 2-inch-long matchsticks

1/4 cup shredded fresh flat-leaf parsley

2 tablespoons shredded fresh mint or cilantro

For the vinaigrette:

2 shallots, minced

1/2 cup extra-virgin olive oil

1/4 cup fresh orange juice

2 tablespoons sherry vinegar

2 teaspoons honey

1 teaspoon ground cumin

1/8 teaspoon paprika

pinch of cayenne pepper

salt and freshly ground pepper to taste

The flavors of Morocco predominate in this crisp salad. Its fresh taste creates a nice balance to the rich ham and adds a sharp jolt of color to the Easter table. For a milder salad, eliminate or reduce the amount of cumin to 1/2 teaspoon, and substitute fresh chives for the mint or cilantro. For easy mixing, measure the vinaigrette ingredients in a jar with a screw-top lid and let your little one shake away.

Serves 8 to 10

Bring a large saucepan filled with lightly salted water to a boil. Add the carrots, bring back to a boil, and cook for 1 minute. Drain the carrots and plunge them immediately into a large bowl of ice water. When completely cool, no more than 5 minutes, drain and dry well. In a large serving bowl, toss together the carrots, parsley, and mint.

To make the vinaigrette, whisk together all the ingredients. Drizzle the vinaigrette over the carrots, parsley, and mint and toss well. Cover and refrigerate for at least 1 hour or up to 1 day. Serve chilled or at room temperature.

see photo on page 34

hot cross buns with dried sour cherries and pistachios

Hot cross buns were traditionally prepared by English housewives on Good Friday. To ward off evil spirits, the buns were marked with a cross made from dough before baking or with icing after baking. Here the recipe is updated with dried sour cherries and pistachios.

Makes 16 buns

Combine 5 tablespoons of the sugar, the milk, butter, cinnamon, nutmeg, cloves, and lemon zest in a small saucepan over medium heat. Stir until the milk is hot and the butter is melted. Remove from the heat and pour into a large bowl. Let cool to room temperature. Meanwhile, combine the warm water with the remaining 1 tablespoon sugar in a small bowl. Sprinkle the yeast over the water and let stand until frothy, about 10 minutes. Whisk the whole egg, the egg yolks, and the yeast into the cooled milk.

In another bowl, stir together the $3\frac{1}{3}$ cups flour and the salt. Add the yeast mixture, stirring until a sticky dough forms. Stir in the sour cherries and pistachios. Turn the dough out onto a lightly floured board or countertop and knead until smooth and elastic, 10 to 15 minutes. If the dough is too sticky, sprinkle with a little more flour.

Transfer to a lightly buttered bowl and brush the surface with a little melted butter. Cover loosely with plastic wrap and let rise in a warm, draft-free place until doubled in bulk, about 2 hours. Punch down and knead briefly. Re-cover and let rise a second time, about 30 minutes. Punch the dough down again and knead briefly. Divide into quarters and divide each quarter into 4 equal pieces. Roll each piece of dough into a smooth ball and place in a lightly buttered 9-by-13-inch pan. Cover loosely with plastic wrap and let rise a final time until doubled, about 30 minutes.

6 tablespoons granulated sugar

1 cup milk

$\frac{1}{4}$ cup ($\frac{1}{2}$ stick) unsalted butter

$\frac{1}{2}$ teaspoon ground cinnamon

$\frac{1}{4}$ teaspoon ground nutmeg

$\frac{1}{8}$ teaspoon ground cloves

grated zest of 1 lemon

$\frac{1}{4}$ cup warm water

2 packages active dry yeast

1 whole egg plus 2 egg yolks

$3\frac{1}{3}$ cups all-purpose unbleached flour, plus more for kneading

1 teaspoon salt

1 cup dried sour cherries

$\frac{1}{2}$ cup chopped pistachios

melted unsalted butter for greasing and brushing

1 egg yolk mixed with 1 tablespoon milk, for glazing

For the icing:

1 cup confectioners' sugar

1 to 2 teaspoons milk, heated

Preheat the oven to 375°F.

Brush the buns with the egg glaze. Bake until golden brown and the buns sound hollow when rapped on the bottom, 20 to 25 minutes. Let cool completely on a wire rack.

To make the icing, combine the confectioners' sugar and 1 teaspoon warm milk in a bowl. Stir until smooth, adding another 1 teaspoon milk if needed to achieve a smooth consistency. Spoon into a lock-top sandwich bag, seal, and snip off the tip of one corner. Squeeze the icing from the bag, piping a cross over each cooled bun. Serve the buns at room temperature.

mimosas

3 to 4 cups fresh orange, blood orange, or tangerine juice, chilled

superfine sugar

1 bottle (750 ml) Champagne or other sparkling wine

Tangy, bubbly, refreshing mimosas are a wonderful, adult way to toast the Easter holiday and celebrate spring. A child-friendly version follows, in case the kids don't want to be left out of the fun.

Serves 6 to 8

Dip the rims of Champagne glasses in orange juice and then in superfine sugar. Allow the sugar to dry for a few minutes. Fill each glass a little over half full with Champagne, and then top off each glass with juice. Serve immediately.

Kid's Mimosas: In plastic champagne glasses, combine equal parts orange juice with ginger ale, lemon-lime soda, or sparkling mineral water.

see photo on page 44

corn bread madeleines with leeks and pecans

Madeleines, small shell-shaped French cakes, have a decidedly American accent here. With a cornmeal batter loaded with native American pecans and hearty sautéed leeks, their dainty form belies a robust mouthful that can stand up to the rich flavor of the ham they accompany. Finicky eaters may prefer the madeleines without the nuts and leeks so try making two batches, one with and one without, and then encourage reluctant tasters to sample one of each. Let your child stir together the wet and dry ingredients and fill the tins.

Makes about 24 madeleines

Preheat the oven to 400° F. Spray madeleine tins with nonstick cooking spray.

Stir together the cornmeal, flour, baking powder, baking soda, salt and pecans in a large bowl. In a separate small bowl, stir together the honey, buttermilk, egg, and 4 tablespoons of the melted butter. Add the remaining 2 tablespoons butter to a small skillet over medium heat, add the leeks and sauté until they are limp and just beginning to brown, 2 to 3 minutes. Stir into the buttermilk mixture. Stir the buttermilk mixture into the cornmeal mixture just until combined. Spoon the batter into the prepared tins, filling each mold two-thirds full.

Bake until firm and golden, 10 to 15 minutes Remove from the oven and turn the madeleines out onto a wire rack. Serve warm.

1 cup yellow cornmeal

1 cup all-purpose flour

2 teaspoons baking powder

$1/2$ teaspoon baking soda

$1/4$ teaspoon salt

$1/2$ cup finely chopped pecans

$1/3$ cup honey

$2/3$ cup buttermilk

1 egg

6 tablespoons ($3/4$ stick) unsalted butter, melted

1 large leek, white and pale green part only, well rinsed and thinly sliced

rhubarb-mango fool

2 to 2½ pounds rhubarb, trimmed and cut into 1-inch pieces

1¼ cups sugar

3 tablespoons orange juice

3 large, ripe mangoes (12 to 16 ounces each)

4 cups heavy cream

1 teaspoon pure vanilla extract

Only the most basic skills are necessary to create this simple, creamy dessert. Ripe mangoes should be firm and heavy, with a sweet perfume, and the skin should be smooth rather than leathery. If the mangoes are too hard, hasten ripening by placing them in a brown paper bag with a ripe banana for a day or two. Kids can help whip the cream. If you don't have a freestanding mixer, place a damp towel on the counter and place the mixing bowl on the towel to eliminate slipping.

Makes 8 to 10 servings

Combine the rhubarb, sugar, and orange juice in a heavy-bottomed stainless-steel saucepan. Bring to a boil over high heat. Cover, reduce the heat to a simmer, and cook, stirring occasionally, until the rhubarb is tender and falling apart, about 30 minutes. Uncover and let cool to room temperature.

Peel the mangoes and slice the flesh from the pits. Place in a blender or food processor with the cooled rhubarb and puree until smooth. Cover and refrigerate until very cold, at least 2 hours or up to 2 days.

Pour the cream and vanilla into a chilled bowl and beat with an electric mixer at medium speed until the cream starts to thicken, about 1 minute. Increase the speed to high and beat until firm (not stiff) peaks form, 3 to 4 minutes. Carefully fold the chilled rhubarb mixture into the cream just until combined.

Spoon into serving glasses and chill until ready to serve.

quick tulip tins

For each tulip tin you will need:

empty, clean soup can (19-ounce size)

cloth tape (optional)

tulips

square scarf, at least 21 inches square

twist-tie

grosgrain or silk ribbon, 12 inches long

Spring's bounty of tulips may leave you with a shortage of vases, but a tall soup can concealed by a pretty silk scarf makes an elegant container. If you don't have a silk scarf, purchase some colorful organza or tulle and use pinking shears to cut 21-inch squares.

Peel away the paper label from the soup can. If desired, affix a strip of cloth tape along the inner rim to protect the tulip stems from the rough edge. Fill the can one third full of water and place the tulips in the can. Make sure the outside of the can is dry. Lay the scarf out flat on a table, and place the can in the center of the scarf. Bring the four corners of the scarf up the sides of the can, and gently secure the scarf around the tulip stems with the twist-tie. Tie the grosgrain ribbon over the twist-tie, finishing with a bow.

eggcup placeholders

If you have a pretty collection of eggcups, you can adorn them with rib-
bons and name cards and serve a simple Easter breakfast of soft-boiled
eggs and buttered toast. If soft-boiled eggs aren't on the menu, use the
variation below to make festive, candy-filled eggcup placeholders or
party favors.

Cut out 8 egg-shaped pieces of cardstock, each about the size of a small chicken egg. Punch a hole in the top of each egg card. Write each guest's name on a card in silver pen. Thread one ribbon through the hole in an egg card and tie to the base of the eggcup, making sure the name faces out. Place beside a plate.

variation: Make name cards as instructed above. Following the instructions for Jelly Bean Bags (page 32), fill 8 squares of netting with candied almonds or small chocolate eggs. Thread each ribbon through a name card and tie the bags closed. Perch each bag in an eggcup and place beside a plate.

For 8 eggcup placeholders
you will need:

scissors

8½-by-11-inch sheet white
    cardstock

⅛-inch-hole paper punch

metallic silver pen

8 lengths ribbon, each 6 inches
    long

8 eggcups

51

easter egg hunt luncheon

Planning an Easter egg hunt is fun for both children and adults. Along with the brightly colored hard-boiled eggs, stuff a variety of colored plastic eggs with candy, coins, and small toys. For a more elaborate party, fill small Easter baskets with candy, stuffed toys, and other Easter treats. Hunting for these treasures will whet appetites, large and small, and this simple menu fills the bill nicely.

Many components of the meal can be prepared at least a day in advance: the dip, pot pies (do not glaze until just before baking), and the orange part of the compote (add the strawberries no more than 2 hours before serving to prevent them from getting soggy). The day of the party, hollow out the cabbage and fill with dip, then scrub the vegetables and arrange in the basket. Add the strawberries to the compote and bake the pot pies. Your Easter lunch will be ready as soon as your intrepid egg hunters return with their baskets brimming with goodies.

peter rabbit's spring onion dip with baby carrots and radishes

Seek out baby carrots and radishes with their leafy tops attached. Kids love to pretend they're Flopsy, Mopsy, and Cottontail while digging into this creamy appetizer. Children can stir the dip while you mince and measure the ingredients.

Serves 6

To make the dip, stir together all the ingredients in a bowl. Cover and chill for at least 1 hour, or up to 2 days.

Place the cabbage, stem side down, on a countertop. Push aside (but do not remove) the larger outer leaves and cut off the top of the cabbage. Using a paring knife, carefully carve out the inner portion of the cabbage to form a bowl. Reserve the carved-out portion for another use. Scrub the carrots and radishes, but do not peel.

Line a flat basket with kale leaves. Spoon the dip into the cabbage and place it in the center of the basket. Surround the cabbage with the scrubbed carrots and radishes.

Serve at once.

For the dip:

1¼ cups sour cream

¾ cup mayonnaise

3 to 4 tablespoons finely minced shallots

2 green onions, white and tender green part only, finely minced

2 tablespoons minced fresh parsley

2 tablespoons minced fresh dill

1 teaspoon salt

½ teaspoon garlic salt

freshly ground pepper to taste

2 or 3 drops Tabasco sauce

1 medium head (3 to 4 pounds) green cabbage, outer leaves still attached

1 pound baby carrots

1 pound radishes

curly kale or purple flowering kale leaves

chicken pot pies

4 boneless, skinless chicken
  breasts, 1 to 1¼ pounds

3 cups canned low-sodium
  chicken broth

6 tablespoons (¾ stick)
  unsalted butter

1 cup diced onion

1 clove garlic, crushed

6 tablespoons all-purpose flour

½ cup heavy cream

3 tablespoons minced fresh dill

½ teaspoon paprika

salt and freshly ground pepper
  to taste

2 cups diced unpeeled red
  potatoes

2 cups diced carrots

1 cup frozen petite peas, thawed
  and well drained

1½ pounds puff pastry, thawed
  in the refrigerator if frozen

1 egg yolk mixed with 1 tablespoon heavy cream or milk, for
  glazing

The hunger pangs of the most ravenous egg hunters will be satisfied by these child-friendly pies. Encourage your young cooks to pick out a few tiny Easter cookie cutters they like at the store, then let them roll out the puff pastry and cut out the garnishes.

Serves 6

Place the chicken in a large, heavy-bottomed saucepan and add the chicken broth. Bring to a boil over high heat, reduce the heat to medium-low, and simmer until the juices run clear when a breast is pierced with a knife, about 15 minutes. Remove the chicken and let cool completely. Strain the broth and return to the saucepan. Cook the stock over medium heat until reduced to 2½ cups. Using your fingers, pull the chicken into bite-sized shreds. Set aside.

Melt the butter in a large, heavy-bottomed saucepan. Add the onion and garlic and sauté until translucent, about 5 minutes. Add the flour and stir over medium heat until the mixture forms a smooth, pale golden paste, about 2 minutes. Whisk in the 2½ cups broth, stirring until smooth. Raise the heat to medium-high, bring to a boil, and cook, stirring constantly, for 1 minute. Stir in the cream. Remove from the heat and stir in the dill and paprika. Season with salt and pepper. Set aside.

Preheat the oven to 400° F.

Bring a large pot of lightly salted water to a boil. Add potatoes and carrots and cook until tender, but not mushy, 5 to 7 minutes. Drain well and fold into the sauce along with the peas and shredded chicken.

Butter six 5-inch disposable aluminum pie pans. Divide the chicken mixture evenly among them. On a lightly floured board, roll out the puff pastry ¼ inch thick. Using a sharp knife or pastry wheel and a

template, cut out six 6-inch rounds. Place a puff pastry circle on top of each pan to cover the filling completely, then firmly pinch the pastry over the lip of the pan to seal it. Reroll any puff pastry scraps and use 1-inch Easter cookie cutters to cut out 6 small flowers, bunnies, or chicks to use as garnishes. (To puff properly, the pastry must be completely chilled and firm. If it has softened slightly, chill the pies and the garnishes for at least 30 minutes before glazing.) Brush the tops of the pot pies with the glaze and attach a puff pastry cutout to the center of each pie. Cut a few steam slits in the pastry, avoiding the garnish.

Place pies on a baking sheet. Bake until the pastry is puffed and golden and the filling is hot and bubbly, 30 to 35 minutes. Serve warm.

sparkling strawberry lemonade

This delicious drink tastes more complicated and alluring than its three simple ingredients would indicate. Kids can stir the ingredients together as you pour them into the pitcher. Serve over ice and garnish each glass with a whole fresh strawberry or a wheel of lemon. For an adult cocktail, stir a shot of vodka or tequila into each glass right before serving.

1 can (12 ounces) frozen lemon-ade concentrate, thawed

2 quarts club soda or other plain sparkling water

½ cup strawberry puree, made from about 1 cup frozen strawberries

ice cubes

Makes about 2 quarts

Combine the thawed lemonade concentrate, club soda, and strawberry puree in a large pitcher. Stir to combine and chill until ready to serve.

To serve, pour over ice in tall glasses.

strawberry-orange compote

A light, refreshing finish to any meal. Children can hull the strawberries while you segment the oranges.

Serves 6

Place the strawberries in a large glass bowl. Working with 1 orange at a time, and using a serrated knife, cut a slice off the top and bottom of the orange to reveal the orange flesh. Stand the orange upright on the cutting board. Then cut off the rind, including the white pith, in wide strips, following the contour of the orange and slicing from the top to the bottom with a light sawing motion. Hold a peeled fruit in one hand over the glass bowl, and use a small, sharp paring knife to cut between the fruit and the tough membrane on either side of each segment to loosen it, letting the segments drop into the bowl. After removing the segments from all the oranges, squeeze the membranes over the bowl, capturing any juices. Discard the membranes.

Combine the ½ cup orange juice and sugar in a small saucepan. Bring to a boil over high heat and cook for 1 minute. Remove from the heat and let cool to room temperature. Drizzle the orange syrup over the orange segments and strawberries and toss to combine.

Cover and refrigerate until very cold, but no more than 3 hours, as the strawberries start to break down. Serve chilled.

2 pints strawberries, hulled and sliced

6 large navel oranges

½ cup fresh orange juice

¼ cup sugar

easter dinner

The regal lamb, the traditional centerpiece of many a Mediterranean Easter feast, is featured in this elegant holiday dinner. Here, a leg is boned and butterflied and drenched in a marinade fragrant with garlic and rosemary, making for a simple and delicious preparation. This is a perfect menu for introducing your children to the abundant produce at its peak in the spring. Included is a creamy risotto laced with grilled asparagus and a delicate salad of baby spinach and spicy watercress with a piquant feta vinaigrette. A heavenly pavlova, filled with whipped cream and topped with fresh strawberries, makes a perfect finale to a menu that celebrates the ancient traditions of the Easter feast and highlights the bounty of the season.

Most of the recipes for this menu should be made on the day of the feast to preserve the freshness of the ingredients. Make the marinade and marinate the lamb up to 24 hours prior to the meal and keep in the refrigerator until it's time for grilling.

grilled butterflied leg of lamb
with garlic and rosemary

1 leg of lamb, 6 to 7 pounds,
boned and butterflied

For the marinade:

¾ cup olive oil

½ cup red wine vinegar

¼ cup balsamic vinegar

⅓ cup minced fresh rosemary

¼ cup minced fresh thyme

2 tablespoons soy sauce

2 teaspoons Worcestershire sauce

2 teaspoons anchovy paste

7 or 8 large cloves garlic,
crushed

kosher salt and freshly ground
pepper to taste

Have your butcher bone and butterfly a leg of lamb. A butterflied leg is usually of uneven thickness, but don't let this bother you. When it is grilled, there will be rare, medium-rare, and medium-well sections to satisfy every palate.

Serves 8

Trim off any excess fat from the lamb and place it in a 9-by-13-inch nonreactive pan. Whisk together all the marinade ingredients in a nonreactive bowl. Scoop out and reserve ¼ cup of the marinade, and pour the remainder over the lamb. Massage into the meat. Cover and refrigerate for 12 to 24 hours.

Remove the meat from the refrigerator and allow to come to room temperature. Prepare a fire in a charcoal grill. The coals are ready when they are an ashen gray with a glowing red center. This will take 30 to 40 minutes. If using a gas grill, preheat to medium heat.

Place the lamb on the grill rack and cook, turning once and basting frequently with the reserved ¼ cup marinade, for 15 to 18 minutes on each side for medium-rare.

Transfer to a platter, season with salt and pepper, and tent with aluminum foil. Let rest for 10 minutes before slicing, then place on a cutting board and slice thinly. Arrange attractively on the platter and pour over any accumulated juices. Serve immediately.

grilled asparagus risotto

This dish is a great introduction to asparagus, often a "difficult" vegetable for kids. The grilling adds a tasty, smoky flavor that may make the spears more palatable to young diners. It is the only way my daughter, Olivia, will eat asparagus.

Serves 6 to 8

Prepare a medium-low fire in a charcoal grill, or preheat a gas grill to medium-low.

Using a vegetable peeler, lightly peel each asparagus spear to within about 2 inches of the tip. Rub the asparagus with the olive oil and season lightly with kosher salt and pepper. Place on the grill rack and grill, turning often, until tender and marked with brown grill marks, 5 to 7 minutes. Be careful not to cook the asparagus over heat that is too high, as high heat inhibits thorough cooking and makes the asparagus bitter. Transfer to a cutting board, let cool slightly, and cut on the diagonal into 1-inch pieces. Set aside.

Pour the stock into a saucepan, place over medium heat, and bring to a boil. Reduce the heat so the stock barely simmers.

Heat the olive oil and 1 tablespoon of the butter in a heavy-bottomed 3-quart saucepan over medium-high heat. Add the shallots and garlic and sauté until translucent, 3 to 4 minutes. Add the rice and cook, stirring often, for 1 minute. Stir in the wine and cook, stirring, until nearly evaporated. Add just enough of the hot stock to cover the rice, about 1 cup. Reduce the heat to maintain a good simmer and cook, stirring continuously. When the stock is absorbed, add more stock, about ½ cup at a time, and stir until incorporated. The rice will plump up and the mixture will become creamier as the risotto cooks. Continue cooking,

For the grilled asparagus:

1 pound medium-sized asparagus

3 tablespoons olive oil

kosher salt and freshly ground pepper to taste

6 to 7 cups homemade chicken stock or canned low-sodium chicken broth

2 tablespoons olive oil

3 tablespoons unsalted butter

2 large shallots, minced

2 cloves garlic, minced

2 cups Arborio rice

⅓ cup dry white wine

½ cup freshly grated pecorino romano cheese

freshly ground pepper to taste

stirring all the while, until all the stock is incorporated and the rice kernels are creamy on the outside and al dente in the center, 25 to 28 minutes total. Stir in the asparagus with the last addition of the stock.

Remove from the heat and add the remaining 2 tablespoons butter and the cheese, stirring until well combined. Season with pepper. Serve immediately.

easter votives

Many grocery and craft stores sell cylindrical votive candles in 8¼-inch-tall glasses. They are quite inexpensive, and they look beautiful wrapped in sheets of natural-fiber paper trimmed with ribbon. Choose papers with some texture or pattern; mulberry bark tissue is especially nice. Buy several votives, cover them in different kinds of paper, and light them at your Easter dinner table. Kids can help measure and cut the papers, tape, and ribbons.

Trim the craft paper to an 8-by-8¾-inch rectangle. Apply an 8½-inch length of double-sided tape to one long edge of the paper. Affix 1 piece of ribbon to the tape, matching the edges. Repeat on the other long edge of the rectangle.

With the ribbon side out and the ribbons running horizontally at the top and bottom, wrap the paper around the votive. Run an 8-inch strip of tape along the short edge of the paper. Overlap the other edge and press to secure. Make sure no paper or ribbon sticks up over the lip of the glass. Light the candle and enjoy.

see photo on page 2

For each candle you will need:

scissors

craft paper, such as mulberry bark tissue, lace paper, or rice paper

double-sided tape, ½ inch wide

2 pieces of ribbon, each 8¼ inches long and 1 inch wide

spinach and watercress salad with feta vinaigrette

Children can rinse the greens and spin them dry in a salad spinner. They can also pour the vinaigrette ingredients into the blender and push the button. If your children turn their noses up at the spinach and watercress, you can substitute crisp romaine lettuce. The bread can go onto the same grill used for the asparagus and lamb.

Serves 6 to 8

To make the vinaigrette, combine the olive oil, vinegars, mustard, honey, and oregano in a blender. Blend until smooth. Pour into a bowl and season with salt and pepper. Stir in the crumbled feta cheese.

To make the croutons, grill the bread over a medium charcoal fire or gas grill, or on a stove-top grill pan, turning once, until browned and crisp on both sides, about 2 minutes on each side. Remove from the grill or grill pan and rub one side of each slice with the garlic clove. Drizzle each bread slice with 1 teaspoon olive oil. Then cut or tear into 1-inch cubes or pieces.

Toss together the spinach leaves, watercress, and red onion in a large salad bowl. Drizzle the feta vinaigrette over the greens and toss well. Top with the croutons and serve immediately.

For the feta vinaigrette:

½ cup olive oil

¼ cup red wine vinegar

2 tablespoons sherry vinegar

1 tablespoon Dijon mustard

1 teaspoon honey

1 teaspoon dried Greek oregano

kosher salt and freshly ground pepper to taste

½ pound feta cheese, crumbled

For the garlic croutons:

3 or 4 slices firm country bread, each ½ inch thick

1 large clove garlic, peeled but left whole

3 or 4 teaspoons olive oil

8 cups loosely packed baby spinach leaves, well rinsed and dried

2 bunches watercress, tough stems removed, well rinsed and dried

½ red onion, sliced paper-thin

little violet vases

For each "stained-glass" vase you will need:

lavender tissue paper

pinking shears or scissors

clean glass jar

gel medium (available in art supply stores)

small paintbrush

newspapers

clear acrylic spray

Nosegays of spring flowers are lovely in little vases. Look for a small-mouthed glass jar, such as a mustard, jam, or small olive container. Soak off the label and dry thoroughly before beginning. Experiment with different colors of tissue paper, and outfit your Easter table with an assortment of cheerful vases filled with a variety of blossoms.

Using the pinking shears or scissors, cut the tissue paper into small pieces of varying sizes (think postage stamps). To make this easier, fold the tissue paper accordion style, snip off strips of varying widths, and then cut across each strip, forming smaller, rectangular pieces.

Gently brush the gel medium onto a tissue paper rectangle, and affix the damp side of the tissue to the jar. Gently brush more gel medium over the tissue paper. Repeat, overlapping the tissue paper pieces and covering the glass completely. Allow to dry. Once dry, the gel medium will be clear.

Cover an outdoor work surface with newspapers, place the jar on top, and spray with the clear acrylic spray. Allow to dry thoroughly. Your jar is now ready for water and flowers. Your vase is not dishwasher safe, however. To wash, rinse the inside gently with warm water and drain dry.

easter sweets
and treats

easter basket cupcakes

3 cups all-purpose flour

2 teaspoons baking powder

1 teaspoon baking soda

1 teaspoon salt

2 teaspoons ground cinnamon

$^1\!/_2$ teaspoon ground ginger

$^1\!/_4$ teaspoon ground nutmeg

1 cup vegetable oil

$^3\!/_4$ cup buttermilk

4 eggs

1 cup granulated sugar

1 cup firmly packed light brown sugar

1 tablespoon pure vanilla extract

1 pound carrots, peeled and grated (about $3^1\!/_2$ cups packed)

2 cups chopped walnuts

1 cup sweetened, shredded coconut

1 cup drained crushed canned pineapple

For the cream cheese icing:

$^1\!/_2$ cup (1 stick) unsalted butter, at room temperature

continued

My mother made these cupcakes for me when I was growing up, and they are just as much fun to make now as they were then. Children can help peel the carrots, measure dry ingredients into a large bowl, and stir together the wet and dry ingredients. Place bowls of icing, coconut, and jelly beans on the table and demonstrate how to construct the first basket. Let the children assemble the rest. They can choose red licorice whips for the basket handle, or try one of the new fruit-flavored whips that come in colors as varied as yellow, orange, and pink.

Makes 24 cupcakes

Preheat the oven to 350° F.

Line 24 standard muffin cups with paper liners.

Sift together the flour, baking powder, baking soda, salt, cinnamon, ginger, and nutmeg into a large bowl. In a separate bowl, whisk together the oil, buttermilk, eggs, granulated and brown sugars, and vanilla until smooth. Stir in the grated carrots, walnuts, coconut, and pineapple. Using a wooden spoon, stir the dry ingredients into the wet ingredients just until combined. Spoon into the lined muffin cups, filling each three-quarters full.

Bake until a toothpick inserted into the center of a cupcake comes out clean, about 25 minutes. Let cool completely on a wire rack.

To make the icing, in a bowl beat together the butter and cream cheese with an electric mixer set at medium speed until light and fluffy. Beat in the orange zest and vanilla. Beat in the confectioners' sugar, 1 cup at a time. Continue beating until light and creamy. You should have about 3 cups.

To color coconut, disolve a few drops of liquid or paste food coloring in 1 teaspoon water. Put coconut in a lock-top plastic bag and dribble dissolved food coloring over it. Seal bag and massage food coloring into the coconut until it is evenly distributed and no white streaks remain.

Spread the cooled cupcakes generously with the icing. Press the coconut onto the icing to resemble Easter basket grass. Press 3 jelly beans into the coconut grass on each cupcake. To create the basket handle, insert one end of a licorice whip into one side of a cupcake. (If you experience difficulty inserting the licorice, pierce the cupcake with the tip of a paring knife to ease the way.) Insert the other end into the opposite side of the cupcake, to form the semicircular handle.

Serve the cupcakes immediately, or cover lightly with plastic wrap and chill for up to 12 hours before serving.

1 package (8 ounces) cream cheese, at room temperature

1 teaspoon grated orange zest

1 teaspoon pure vanilla extract

4 cups (1 pound) confectioners' sugar, sifted

For decorating:

3 cups coconut

liquid or paste food coloring

72 jelly beans, in assorted colors

24 red licorice or other fruit-flavored whips

paint a bunny face

Children love to have their faces painted. Here's a simple way to make bunnies out of your little ones. If you want to get more elaborate, purchase a set of water-based face paints and set up a face-painting station at the Easter egg hunt.

Using the paintbrush or the brush from the liquid eyeliner, draw an upside down triangle on the child's nose. Fill in completely. Rub a circle of rouge, or paint a circle, on each cheek. Paint 3 whiskers on each side of the face, starting below each nostril and extending across the cheek.

To paint a bunny face you will need:

small paintbrush (if using face paint)

brown or black liquid eyeliner or water-based face paint

pink powder rouge or water-based face paint

1 pound (4 sticks) unsalted
  butter, at room temperature

1¼ cups granulated sugar

1 tablespoon pure vanilla extract

4½ cups all-purpose flour

1 teaspoon salt

For the royal icing:

2 egg whites, or 4 tablespoons
  meringue powder mixed with
  ½ cup warm water

4 cups (1 pound) confectioners'
  sugar

water for thinning

paste food coloring in various
  colors

colored sugar crystals, sanding
  sugar, sprinkles, candy dots,
  and/or small sugared flowers
  (page 31)

Adults and children will enjoy cutting out and decorating these charming Easter bonnet cookies. To streamline the process, prepare the cookies beforehand—they freeze well for up to 2 weeks. Let the kids ice and adorn their cookies with a variety of decorations, from sanding sugars to sugared flowers.

Makes about 24 cookies

Combine the butter and granulated sugar in a large bowl. Beat together with an electric mixer set at medium-high speed for about 1 minute. Scrape down the sides of the bowl and continue beating until light and fluffy. Beat in the vanilla extract. Sift together the flour and salt. Blend into the butter mixture, 1 cup at a time. Continue mixing until the dough is smooth and no streaks of flour remain. Divide the dough into 4 equal portions. Pat each portion into a disk and wrap in plastic wrap. Refrigerate for 30 minutes.

Working with 1 disk at a time (leave the others chilling), place it between 2 pieces of waxed paper (or plastic wrap) and roll out ¼ inch thick. Remove the top piece of waxed paper, and using a 3-inch scalloped or straight-edged biscuit or cookie cutter, cut out at least 6 cookies. Place the cookies at least 1 inch apart on parchment-lined baking sheets. Reserve the dough scraps. Repeat with the remaining dough disks. Reroll all the scraps and cut out at least 24 smaller cookies with a 1-inch straight-edged cookie cutter.

The smaller cookies will be the crown of the bonnets and the larger cookies will be the brims.

Place on a second parchment-lined baking sheet at least 1-inch apart. Refrigerate both baking sheets until the cookies until very firm and

cold, at least 2 hours or up to 2 days. (If chilling longer than 2 hours, cover loosely with plastic wrap.)

Preheat the oven to 300° F.

Bake the cookies until firm and sandy gold, about 20 minutes. Do not allow them to get too dark, as they can taste slightly bitter if overly browned. Let cool completely on a wire rack before icing.

To make the icing, in a large bowl, beat the egg whites (or reconstituted meringue powder) with an electric mixer set on low speed until frothy. Sift the confectioners' sugar into the bowl. Increase the mixer speed to high and continue beating until brilliant white, firm, and fluffy, about 10 minutes. You should have 2½ to 3 cups. Scoop out 1 cup of the icing and set aside to use for piping.

Thin the remaining icing with water, adding 2 or 3 teaspoons at a time until it is of pouring consistency. Divide the icing among as many small bowls as different colors you wish to create, then tint the portions. Place the cookies on a wire rack set over a baking sheet and pour the thinned icing over them. If necessary, shake the cookies to ease the icing over the edges. This should cover the cookies with a thin, even layer. Allow to dry completely.

Tint the reserved 1 cup icing, if desired. Spoon into a large piping bag fitted with a number 2 plain decorating tip for squiggles, dots, scrolls, and stripes or a number 4 or 5 plain tip, or small petal tip for piping a ribbon. To create the bonnet, pipe a small amount of icing on the back of the smaller cookie and attach it onto the center of the larger cookie.

The bonnets can be decorated in a variety of ways:

* Pipe an icing ribbon and bow around the 1-inch cookie.

* Pipe a series of small icing dots to resemble dotted Swiss, or pipe decorative scrolls or stripes.

* Sprinkle the icing decorations with sanding sugar while they are still wet to make them sparkle.

* Pipe dabs of icing and attach small sugared flowers.

* For a paisley look, pipe or spoon drops of a contrasting color of the thinned icing randomly over the surface of an iced cookie while it is still wet. Using a bamboo skewer or toothpick, pull through the center of each dot.

* For an elegant all-white cookie, ice with white icing and decorate with small dots of white icing to resemble dotted Swiss. "Tie" the bonnet with a white icing ribbon and garnish with a sugared violet.

* Decorate iced cookies with sprinkles and/or candy dots.

Allow the cookies to dry for at least 2 hours, and if the weather is humid, overnight, before packaging.

peter cottontail finger puppet

Felt is a great fabric for crafting. It comes in a rainbow of colors, it doesn't require hemming, and it can be glued as well as sewn. Set out a tray of beads, sequins, and other trimmings for children to glue onto their puppets. For faster finger puppets, use a glue gun instead of craft glue, but be sure to supervise its use. For even easier puppets, simply snip the fingers off of an old cotton glove and decorate the fingertips.

Place the length of your index finger (or your child's finger) on the white felt and, with a fabric pen or pencil, trace loosely around your finger from the very bottom, over the tip, and back down to the bottom. Remove your finger and draw a second line around the first line, approximately 1/3 inch outside of the original line. Cut around this second line and straight across the bottom. Use this cut piece as a template to cut a second, identical piece.

Squeeze a thin line of glue along the edge of your first piece of felt, making sure you are putting it outside of the finger outline. Press the second piece of felt over the first. Allow to dry thoroughly, about 1 hour.

Photocopy or trace the bunny head on this page and cut out the template. Cut away the inside "lining" of the ears. Place the template on the white felt and, using the fabric pen or pencil, trace around the outline of the head. Place the template on the pink felt and, using the fabric pen or pencil, trace around the inside of the ears. Cut out the head and the pink ear "linings." Glue the "lining" onto the ears.

Stitch colored thread onto the bunny face and decorate with wiggle eyes, sequins, beads, scraps of felt, and other adornments. Glue the bunny head onto the tip of the finger puppet form. Glue the cotton ball or white pom-pom to the back of the puppet. Allow to dry before using.

For each finger puppet you will need:

8½-by-11-inch sheet white felt
fabric pen or pencil
craft glue
bunny template (see this page)
8½-by-11-inch sheet pink felt
sewing needle and colored thread
2 wiggle eyes
1 cotton ball or white pom-pom

flaky hens' nests

1 box (7 ounces) Special-K or other toasted rice flakes cereal (about 6 cups)

3 tablespoons unsalted butter

1 package (10 ounces) large marshmallows (about 40)

vegetable shortening or nonstick cooking spray

48 jelly beans or candy-coated chocolate eggs

These are easy versions of the all-time favorite puffed rice treats. Let your kids pour out the cereal while you melt the marshmallows. Once the ingredients are combined, the kids will love shaping the sticky cereal mixture into nests and filling them with candies. The nests will keep for up to 3 days, if wrapped well in waxed paper or plastic wrap.

Makes about 18 nests

Pour the cereal into a large bowl and set aside. Melt the butter in a large saucepan over medium heat. Add marshmallows and stir until completely melted. Remove from the heat and pour over the cereal. Quickly and gently stir together until the cereal is completely coated with the marshmallow mixture.

Rub your hands with vegetable shortening, or spray with nonstick coating spray. Using about 1/3 cup of the cereal mixture for each nest, mold about 18 free-form nest shapes, leaving a depression in the center of each one. Place 3 jelly beans or chocolate eggs in each depression; the nests must still be slightly warm to ensure the candies "stick." Let the nests cool completely on a baking sheet. Wrap each nest individually in waxed paper or plastic wrap.

chicken little cookie pops

From corn dogs to cotton candy, food on a stick spells fun for kids. These lemon-scented chicken-shaped cookies are flaky and tender, with an easy white-chocolate icing and an eye-catching sugary exterior reminiscent of Easter's infamous marshmallow Peeps.

Makes about 24 cookies

Combine the butter and sugar in a large bowl. Beat with an electric mixer set at medium-high speed for 1 minute. Scrape down the sides of the bowl and continue beating until light and fluffy. Beat in the lemon zest, egg yolks, and the vanilla and lemon extracts. Sift together the flour and salt. Blend into the butter mixture, 1 cup at a time. Continue mixing until the dough is smooth and no streaks of flour remain. Divide the dough into 2 equal portions. Pat each portion into a disk and wrap in plastic wrap. Refrigerate for 30 minutes.

Working with 1 disk at a time (leave the other one chilling), place it between 2 pieces of waxed paper (or plastic wrap) and roll out ³/₄ inch thick. Remove the top piece of waxed paper and, using a 3- to 4-inch chicken-shaped cookie cutter, cut out as many cookies as possible. Reserve the dough scraps. Place the cookies at least 2 inches apart on parchment-lined baking sheets. Repeat with the remaining dough disk and then with all the scraps. Carefully insert the top 2 inches of a lollipop stick into the bottom of each cookie, leaving a 4-inch handle. Cover loosely with plastic wrap and refrigerate until the cookies are cold and very firm, at least 2 hours or up to 2 days.

Preheat the oven to 325° F.

Place the cookies in the oven. Immediately reduce the heat to 300° F and bake until firm and pale golden brown, 24 to 28 minutes. Let cool completely on a wire rack before icing.

1 cup (2 sticks) unsalted butter, at room temperature

1¼ cups granulated sugar

1 tablespoon grated lemon zest

4 egg yolks

1 teaspoon pure vanilla extract

1 teaspoon pure lemon extract

3½ cups all-purpose flour

1 teaspoon salt

24 lollipop sticks, each 6 inches long and ⅛ inch in diameter

1 package (12 ounces) white chocolate morsels

1 teaspoon vegetable shortening

sanding sugar in pink, purple, yellow, blue, and green (available in most grocery stores)

Place the white chocolate morsels and the shortening in a heatproof bowl over barely simmering water or in microwave-safe bowl. Heat or microwave, stirring as needed, until melted and smooth.

Using a small, flexible icing spatula, spread a thin layer of melted white chocolate over the entire surface of a cookie, front and back. Hold the cookie over a large plate or the sink and sprinkle generously with a single shade of sanding sugar. The cookie should be completely covered for a vibrant effect. Carefully place the cookie on a baking sheet lined with waxed paper and allow to dry completely. Repeat with the remaining cookies and chocolate.

fuzzy chicks

It takes only minutes to make these adorable chicks. All you need is some craft foam and pom-poms, both available at art supply or craft stores. You will have to wield the needle and the glue gun, but the little ones can select the pom-poms and cut out the base and beak.

Using the needle and thread, stitch the small pom-pom to the large pom-pom. Tie off the ends. Photocopy or trace the base and beak on this page and cut out the templates. Place the templates on the orange craft foam, trace around them, and cut out the base and beak. Glue the bottom of the large pom-pom to the base. Glue the beak to the small pom-pom. Glue the wiggle eyes above the beak.

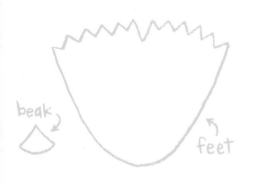

For each fuzzy chick you will need:

sewing needle and yellow thread

yellow pom-pom, 1-inch diameter

yellow pom-pom, 2-inch diameter

base and beak templates (see this page)

pen or pencil

8½-by-11-inch sheet orange craft foam

glue gun

2 wiggle eyes

easter bunny cake

1 standard white cake mix

3 cups cream cheese icing (page 70)

1 cup (6 ounces) white chocolate morsels

2 blue, pink, or black jelly beans or Junior Mints

1 mini marshmallow

1 large marshmallow

red or black licorice strings, cut into six 4-inch lengths

cornstarch for rolling

5 ounces ready-to-use rolled fondant (for the ears)

pesticide-free fresh or sugared flowers (optional, page 31)

2 sheets tissue paper

This three-dimensional lop-eared bunny cake is ambitious, but a lot of fun to make. Color your bunny pink—or any other color you like—by coloring the icing and white chocolate with food coloring. Color the white chocolate with oil-or powder-based food coloring to prevent it from clumping. The chocolate shavings can be prepared a few days in advance, and stored in an airtight container in the refrigerator. For quick-and-easy fur, use shredded sweetened coconut instead of chocolate shavings. Either way, make sure to pat on while the icing is fresh. If you wait too long, the icing will form a crust and the fur won't stick.

Makes 1 bunny cake

Make the cake batter and divide among one 9-inch round cake pan and two 6-inch round cake pans. Bake as directed and let cool completely on a wire rack.

Using a long, serrated knife, cut the 9-inch cake round in half to form 2 half-moons. Spread the top of 1 half-moon with about 1/3 cup icing and sandwich the halves together. Place on a 12-inch round or oval platter, cut side down. This will be the bunny's body. Using a small offset spatula, frost the body with a very thin coat of icing to seal the cake.

For the bunny haunches, cut one of the 6-inch cake rounds in half to form 2 half-moons. Stand 1 half-moon on its cut side so the rounded side is on top. Cut a small V-shaped notch from the far right of the rounded cake top to create a rabbit haunch. Repeat with the second half of the cake. Attach one haunch to either side of the bunny cake body with a little frosting, and give each haunch a thin coat of icing to seal the cake.

Using a 4-inch round biscuit cutter, cut out a round from the remaining 6-inch cake layer. (Or create a cardboard template and carefully cut from the cake with a serrated knife.) This will be the bunny head. From the remaining cake, cut out a 2-inch round for the tail. (If it isn't perfectly round, don't worry; it will be covered with frosting.)

On the bunny body, slice a narrow sliver of cake 2 inches from the center of the rounded top, going toward the bottom of the cake, to form a ledge for the bunny head. Spread the 4-inch cake round with a thin coating of icing and place in this ledge. Give the 2-inch tail a thin coating and press onto the back of the body, resting it on the plate. Frost the entire cake with a thicker coating of icing, covering completely, but allowing the indentations of the bunny's form to remain distinct.

Place the white chocolate morsels in a heatproof bowl placed over barely simmering water or in a microwave-safe bowl. Heat or microwave until smooth, stirring as needed. Pour the chocolate out onto the back of a large aluminum baking sheet or onto the inside bottom of a rimless baking sheet. Using a long (12-inch) offset, or icing spatula, spread the chocolate evenly about 1/16 inch thick. Let firm up, but not become completely hard, about 5 minutes. Place the baking sheet on a countertop and brace it against your body. Hold the blade of an 8-inch long metal icing spatula in both hands and scrape the chocolate off the pan, toward you, in large curls. As the white chocolate continues to harden, the curls will break and become large shards. This is fine, as the white chocolate fur looks great when it contains different sizes of curls and shards. Your cake will resemble a fluffy angora bunny.

Press white chocolate curls and shards all over the bunny's face, body, and tail to form the fur.

Press the 2 jelly beans or Junior Mints into the face for the eyes. Use a mini marshmallow for the nose. Cut 1 large marshmallow in half and press the cut sides into the frosting right under the nose to form cheeks. Pierce each marshmallow cheek with three 4-inch licorice lengths to form the whiskers (if necessary, pierce holes in the marsh-mallow cheeks to ease the way for the whiskers).

To make the bunny ears, dust a work surface and rolling pin with cornstarch. Knead the fondant until smooth and pliable, and roll out into a 10-inch round. Cut out a cardboard template of a 6-to 7-inch bunny ear, with a nice pointed tip and squared-off bottom. Or be dar-ing and cut the ear free-hand. Using a sharp paring knife or pizza wheel, cut the ear out of the fondant. Lay the first fondant ear over the remaining rolled-out fondant, trace a second ear, and cut it out. Discard any remaining fondant. Carefully pinch the squared-off end of an ear together and position the ear—pinched corners face down—on the head to resemble a lop-eared rabbit. I find it is best to pierce a small indentation near the center of the top of the bunny's head to position the ear. Attach the second ear, leaving a $\frac{1}{4}$-inch space between them. Pinching the ends of the ears gives them a little height and helps them better resemble the real thing. If using, place 1 or 2 fresh or sugared flowers in the space between the ears for balance and decoration. To prevent the ears from drying flat, and to give them a little expression, crumple tissue paper into a ball and position it between the drooping ear and the side of the cake. Allow to dry com-pletely before removing the tissue.

If using, surround the base of the bunny cake with fresh or sugared flowers to give the illusion that the bunny is sitting in a flower bed.

white chocolate truffles

The mellow flavor of white chocolate makes these truffles the perfect addition to any Easter basket. They were inspired by a recipe for dark chocolate truffles created by Nick Malgieri, a well-known pastry chef and cookbook author. You may substitute kirsch, framboise, or amaretto for the Grand Marnier, if you like.

Makes 32 truffles

To make the ganache, place the chocolate in a large heatproof bowl. In a saucepan over medium-low heat, combine the cream, butter, and corn syrup. Stir until the butter melts and bubbles start to form on the cream around the edges of the pan (about 120° to 130° F). Pour the hot cream mixture over the chopped chocolate and let stand without stirring for 30 seconds, then stir until smooth and creamy and thoroughly combined. Stir in the Grand Marnier. Chill for 10 minutes. Remove from the refrigerator and beat with an electric mixer set at high speed for 2 minutes to lighten. Return to the refrigerator and chill for 30 to 45 minutes. Use a miniature ice cream scoop (about 1 tablespoon) or melon baller to form mounds of ganache, placing them on a baking sheet lined with waxed paper or parchment paper. Chill until cold and very firm, at least 1 hour or up to 12 hours.

To prepare the coating, combine the chocolate morsels and vegetable shortening in a heatproof bowl placed over barely simmering water or in a microwave-safe bowl. Heat or microwave, stirring as needed, until melted and smooth. Assemble all the garnish ingredients in separate bowls. Working with one mound at a time, dip it in the melted morsels, turning it with one hand, to ensure it is completely covered. You can also use a fork instead of your hand to roll each mound in the melted morsels.

For the ganache filling:

1 pound fine-quality white chocolate such as Callebaut or Lindt, coarsely chopped

½ cup plus 3 tablespoons heavy cream

1 tablespoon unsalted butter

2 teaspoons light corn syrup

2 tablespoons Grand Marnier

For the coating:

1 package (12 ounces) white chocolate baking morsels

1 teaspoon vegetable shortening

For garnish:

½ cup finely chopped pistachios, (optional)

pastel-colored jimmies or sprinkles

sugared pansies or violets (page 31)

1 cup sweetened, shredded coconut, toasted (see note)

white chocolate baking morsels, melted and tinted, for drizzling

Place on a baking sheet lined with waxed paper. Use your chocolate-covered hand or the fork to drizzle a little design of melted chocolate over the truffle. Use your clean hand to sprinkle with pistachios or jimmies (or sprinkles), or to place a sugared flower on the top. Alternatively, dip the mound in melted chocolate morsels and then drop it into the bowl of coconut and, using your clean hand, roll to coat the truffle completely. Place the coconut truffle on waxed paper to set the coating completely. Repeat with the remaining truffles and garnishes. You can also color melted white morsels with powdered- or oil-based food coloring in pastel shades of green, yellow, pink, or violet, and drizzle with a fork over plain white-dipped truffles. With so many truffles, it's nice to see a variety of garnishes, especially if you will be giving them as gifts.

Store the truffles in a tightly covered container. They can be refrigerated for up to 1 week. (Sugared flower decorations may wilt from the moisture in the refrigerator.) They can also be stored, tightly covered, in a cool, dark place for up to 2 days.

note: Toasted coconut is crisp and richly flavored. To toast, spread coconut evenly over a large, ungreased baking sheet. Bake for 5 to 10 minutes in at 350°F, stirring occasionally, until crisp and golden.

easter collage box

Here is a wonderful container in which to present your homemade truffles or other Easter treats. Small cardboard or wooden boxes are readily available at most craft stores. Children will enjoy choosing and snipping small images from wrapping paper, wallpaper samples, greeting cards, or magazines. Using decorative stickers is particularly easy for very young children. Create an elaborate collage or sponge-paint the box with water-based paint and glue on just a few images. Before applying the acrylic spray, have your young artist sign and date the bottom of the box. (If the bottom is a little messy, glue on a piece of art paper and then sign.)

Carefully cut out all the pictures and images you will need for the project before proceeding. Store them in a lock-top bag until you are ready to begin gluing.

Brush or sponge a light coat of paint over the outside of a cardboard or wooden box of your choice. Allow the box to dry thoroughly. Using a small paintbrush, brush the underside of the image and the place on the box where it will go with glue and adhere the image to the box. Rub a barely damp sponge over the picture to remove any wrinkles and excess glue. Repeat with the remaining cutouts to create a collage effect, or just a few special images. (Stickers, of course, make this job very easy and are a good idea for very young children.) Once the images are in place and the box is completely dry, brush the outside of the box with a coat or two of glue (drying thoroughly after each layer), or for a firmer, shinier finish, take the box outside and spray the outside with clear acrylic spray. Allow to dry thoroughly—at least overnight—before filling with Easter treats.

see photo on page 86

For each collage box you will need:

small, sharp scissors

wallpaper samples, wrapping paper, greeting cards, or decorative stickers with flowers, bunnies, eggs, birds, baskets, and other Easter themes

small paintbrushes and sponges

water-based craft paint

small oval, square, rectangular, egg-, or heart-shaped cardboard or wooden boxes (readily available in various sizes at most craft stores)

découpage glue

clear gloss polyurethane spray (optional)

pavlova

cornstarch for the baking sheet, plus 5 teaspoons

5 egg whites, at room temperature

$\frac{1}{8}$ teaspoon cream of tartar

pinch of salt

$1\frac{1}{2}$ cups superfine sugar

$1\frac{1}{2}$ teaspoons distilled white vinegar

1 teaspoon pure vanilla extract

For the filling:

2 cups heavy cream

6 to 8 tablespoons granulated sugar

2 teaspoons pure vanilla extract

1 pint strawberries, hulled and sliced

3 kiwifruits, peeled and sliced

This cloudlike confection is believed to have been created in Australia to commemorate a visit by the famous Russian ballerina, Anna Pavlova. With its crisp exterior and soft, marshmallowy interior, the Pavlova epitomizes the perfect Easter dessert: sweetness and light and revolving around the eternal egg. Children can hull the berries and try separating eggs, but they need to be careful that absolutely no yolk ends up in the whites. Swirling the raw meringue into a shell is a fun, simple task that will encourage younger kids to try this lovely dessert.

Makes 8 to 10 servings

Preheat the oven to 300° F. Line a baking sheet with parchment paper and sprinkle lightly with cornstarch.

Rinse a large stainless-steel bowl under hot water to warm it. Dry well and add the egg whites and cream of tartar. Using an electric mixer at medium-high speed, beat the whites until they begin to turn opaque. Add the salt and continue beating until the whites are firm, but not dry. Continue beating, adding $1\frac{1}{4}$ cups of the superfine sugar, 1 tablespoon at a time, beating for about 10 seconds after each addition. Combine the 5 teaspoons cornstarch with the last $\frac{1}{4}$ cup sugar and continue adding to the egg whites, 1 tablespoon at a time, beating 10 seconds after each addition. Add the vinegar and vanilla and continue beating until the mixture is very glossy and stiff, 1 to 2 minutes longer.

Scoop all the meringue onto the prepared baking sheet. Using a large offset, or icing, spatula, spread the meringue into an 8-inch round, building up the sides and creating a depression in the center. There is no need to make the surface perfectly smooth. The mounds and swirls contribute to its free-form appeal.

Place in the oven and immediately reduce the heat to 250° F. Bake, without opening the oven door, for 1½ hours. Turn off the oven, and crack the oven door slightly. Leave in the oven for an additional 30 minutes. Remove from the oven and let cool completely on a rack. Use a large metal spatula to transfer the meringue to a serving platter.

Up to 1 hour before serving, do the final assembly: Combine the cream, granulated sugar, and vanilla in a chilled bowl and beat with an electric mixer at medium speed until the cream starts to thicken, about 1 minute. Increase the speed to high and continue beating until firm peaks form, 3 to 4 minutes. Fill the center of the meringue with the whipped cream and top with the sliced berries and kiwifruits.

ivory "eggshells" with lemon cream

Both children and adults will be charmed by these duck egg-sized chocolate shells filled with tart, lemony mousse. Let the kids assist in blowing up the balloons and coating them in chocolate.

For the lemon cream:

9 eggs

1½ cups sugar

1 cup fresh lemon juice

2 tablespoons grated lemon zest

½ cup (1 stick) unsalted butter, at room temperature, cut into tablespoon-sized pieces

2 cups heavy cream

6 small, round balloons (size 5)

2 bags (12 ounces each) white chocolate morsels

nonstick cooking spray

Serves 6

To make the lemon cream, combine the eggs, sugar, lemon juice, and zest in a heatproof bowl placed over (not touching) simmering water. Whisk continuously until thickened, 8 to 10 minutes. Whisk in the butter, 1 tablespoon at a time. Transfer to a cool bowl and press a sheet of plastic wrap directly onto the surface to prevent a skin from forming. Refrigerate until very cold, at least 2 hours or up to 12 hours.

To complete the lemon cream, pour the cream into a chilled bowl and beat with an electric mixer at medium speed until it starts to thicken, about 1 minute. Increase the speed to high and continue beating until firm peaks form, 3 to 4 minutes. Remove the plastic wrap from the lemon cream base and fold in one-third of the cream to loosen it up. Fold the remaining cream into the lemon base just until no white streaks remain. Cover and chill until ready to fill the chocolate shells.

To make the "eggshells," line a baking sheet with parchment or waxed paper. Blow the balloons up until they are approximately 4 inches high and 6 to 7 inches in diameter. Knot the balloons and rinse under cool water. Dry thoroughly. Set aside.

Place half of the chocolate morsels in a heatproof bowl over (not touching) barely simmering water. Heat, stirring occasionally, until melted and smooth.

Spray 1 balloon lightly with nonstick cooking spray. Hold the balloon by the knot and dip and roll the balloon in the melted chocolate until

it is evenly coated. Hold the balloon upright over the bowl and allow any excess chocolate to drip off. Position the balloon firmly, standing upright, on the lined baking sheet and refrigerate. Repeat with the remaining balloons, melting more chocolate morsels as needed and immediately placing each balloon in the refrigerator. Refrigerate until the coating is very hard, 1 to 2 hours.

To remove the balloons, grasp a knot firmly and pierce the balloon with a pin. Hang on to the knot and carefully pull the deflating balloon away from the sides of the eggshell. Discard the balloon. Spoon the lemon cream into a large pastry bag fitted with a large, plain tip. Carefully pipe the lemon cream in the eggshells, filling to within 1 to 2 inches of the top. Using your fingers, carefully break and pick at the top of the shell to give it a just-cracked look. Serve immediately or refrigerate for a few hours before serving.

garden bunny

Here is a simple spring outing for you and a young rock hound. Pack some snacks and set off in search of a smooth oval rock. It can be small or large, and any color—it just needs to be smooth. Bring it home, wash with soap and water, and allow to dry before painting.

For each garden bunny you will need:

smooth oval rock

small paintbrush

black acrylic paint

newspapers

clear acrylic spray (optional)

Set the rock on a flat surface. Paint a small triangular nose at front end of the rock. Paint two ears stretching back over the top of the rock. Add eyes and whiskers as desired. Allow to dry.

If desired, take the rock outside, set it on newspapers, and spray with clear acrylic spray. Allow to dry thoroughly before nestling the rock in a corner of the garden or in a potted plant.

ribbon wind catcher

For each wind catcher you
will need:

assorted ribbons, 12 inches to 24
   inches long

pinking shears

scissors

heavy, decorative craft paper, at
   least 18 inches long (look for
   pretty and unusual paper at a
   paper or craft store)

glue

2 paperclips (optional)

$\frac{1}{8}$-inch-hole paper punch

ribbon or string for hanging

*A breezy Easter day will send this colorful wind catcher fluttering in
the currents. To make the project less expensive, use strips of colored
crepe paper instead of ribbon.*

Trim one end of each ribbon with the pinking shears.

Cut a 4-by-18-inch strip from the sheet of paper and fold it in half
lengthwise. Unfold and spread the bottom half with glue. Affix the
plain ends of the ribbon to the glued portion of the paper, with the
pinked ends trailing straight down. Spread the top half of the paper
with glue and fold down over the bottom half, hiding the plain ribbon
ends. Bring the ends of the paper together, forming a circle. Overlap
the ends and glue to secure. You can use paperclips to hold the circle
together until it's dry.

When the glue has dried, punch 2 holes on either side of the circle,
thread with ribbon or string, and tie to secure, forming a hanging loop.
Hang the wind catcher in a breezy spot and watch it flutter.

index